CALEB ROSS

Software Architecture patterns for Serverless computing

Contents

Introduction: The Shift to Serverless Computing

The Evolution of Cloud Architectures

In the early days of software development, companies relied on physical servers to run their applications. This era, marked by hardware-centric operations, demanded significant capital investments and technical expertise to manage. The infrastructure was rigid, costly, and labor-intensive, often requiring dedicated teams to maintain, scale, and secure the servers.

However, the rise of cloud computing revolutionized this landscape. Instead of purchasing and managing physical servers, businesses began renting infrastructure from cloud providers. This introduced Infrastructure-as-a-Service (IaaS), where developers could easily deploy their applications without needing to worry about hardware. The pay-as-you-go model of IaaS allowed companies to scale more flexibly, reducing upfront costs. This was followed by Platform-as-a-Service (PaaS), where developers could build and deploy applications without managing the underlying infrastructure.

As applications became more distributed and microservice-based, developers sought even more abstraction and flexibility. Serverless computing was the next logical step. It provided the ultimate abstraction—developers could focus solely on code while the cloud provider managed everything else. The need to provision, scale, or manage servers was eliminated, and the event-driven nature of serverless allowed for more efficient resource utilization.

Why Serverless? Benefits and Trade-offs

Serverless computing introduces a radical shift in how developers think about building and deploying applications. At its core, serverless architecture enables developers to focus on their business logic, abstracting away infrastructure management.

Key Benefits

- **No Server Management**: The most significant advantage of serverless is the elimination of server management. Developers no longer have to worry about provisioning, maintaining, or scaling servers. This responsibility is shifted to the cloud provider, allowing teams to focus purely on application logic.

- **Automatic Scaling**: In a traditional setup, scaling involves configuring servers and handling load balancers to ensure the application can handle increased traffic. With serverless, this is automatic. Functions scale independently based on demand, which makes handling unpredictable traffic patterns easier.

- **Cost Efficiency**: Serverless follows a pay-per-execution pricing model, meaning businesses only pay for what they use. Unlike traditional architectures, where idle servers still incur costs, serverless eliminates wasted resources. This model makes it particularly appealing for startups and small businesses with fluctuating workloads.

- **Event-Driven Architecture**: Serverless is inherently event-driven, making it ideal for applications that respond to triggers like database changes, HTTP requests, or file uploads. This model encourages decoupling services, allowing for highly scalable and flexible architectures.

Key Trade-offs

Despite the benefits, serverless computing also comes with trade-offs that must be carefully considered.

- **Cold Starts**: One of the most common issues in serverless architectures is the "cold start" problem. When a function hasn't been invoked for a while, it may take longer to initialize, leading to increased latency. Although cloud providers are continuously improving, this is still a critical factor for latency-sensitive applications.
- **Vendor Lock-in**: With serverless, applications often become tightly coupled with the cloud provider's services and infrastructure. This can create challenges if a business wants to migrate to another provider in the future. Developers must carefully evaluate whether the benefits of serverless outweigh this risk.
- **Limited Control**: Serverless environments provide limited control over infrastructure. While this can be an advantage in reducing complexity, it can also limit customization options. Applications that require fine-tuned performance optimization may struggle within the constraints of serverless platforms.
- **Testing and Debugging Challenges**: Since the infrastructure is abstracted away, testing and debugging serverless applications can be more complicated, especially in production-like environments. Tools and strategies must be adapted to handle the stateless and distributed nature of serverless architectures.

Purpose of This Book

This book is designed to provide a comprehensive guide to serverless computing, specifically focusing on architecture patterns that allow developers and architects to design robust, scalable, and cost-effective applications. As serverless continues to grow in popularity, it's essential to understand the principles and patterns that make it successful, along with the potential challenges and how to overcome them.

Many books focus solely on the technical aspects of serverless—such as how to deploy a function or configure an API Gateway. However, this book goes beyond that by diving into the architectural patterns that help unlock the full potential of serverless environments. By the end, readers will have a solid understanding of how to design, implement, and optimize serverless architectures using a variety of patterns and tools.

This book is written for software architects, developers, and engineers who want to master the nuances of serverless architectures and apply them to real-world projects. Whether you're migrating an existing application to a serverless model or designing one from scratch, this book provides the foundational knowledge you need.

How to Use This Book

The structure of this book is designed to guide you from the basics of serverless computing to more advanced architectural patterns. Each chapter builds upon the previous one, gradually introducing new concepts, challenges, and solutions.

- **Chapter Overviews**: Each chapter begins with a high-level overview of the key concepts it covers, followed by detailed explanations, real-world examples, and code snippets. Where applicable, diagrams and flowcharts help visualize complex ideas.
- **Case Studies and Examples**: Throughout the book, you'll find case studies that demonstrate the practical application of serverless architecture patterns. These examples are drawn from a range of industries, providing insights into how serverless is being used to solve real-world problems.
- **Hands-On Tutorials**: At the end of many chapters, you'll find step-by-step tutorials to help you implement the concepts covered. These tutorials will guide you through building serverless components and patterns using popular cloud platforms like AWS Lambda, Azure Functions, and Google Cloud Functions.
- **Key Takeaways**: Each chapter concludes with a summary of the key lessons learned. These sections are intended to reinforce the most important points and serve as quick reference material as you apply serverless architectures in your projects.

Overview of the Chapters

This book is divided into 15 chapters, each focusing on a specific aspect of serverless architecture. Here's a brief overview of what to expect:

- **Chapter 1: Understanding Serverless Computing Basics**: We begin with the fundamentals—what serverless computing is, its core components, and how it fits into the broader cloud landscape.
- **Chapter 2: Introduction to Software Architecture Patterns**: Before diving into serverless-specific patterns, we'll review the essential architectural design patterns and principles that lay the groundwork for effective serverless systems.
- **Chapter 3: Event-Driven Architectures**: We explore how serverless functions can be triggered by events and how to design event-driven systems using serverless platforms.
- **Chapter 4: Microservices in Serverless Computing**: This chapter examines how serverless architectures lend themselves to microservices, along with best practices for managing inter-service communication.
- **Chapter 5: API Gateway Design Patterns**: Here, we look at how to design, manage, and secure APIs using serverless components like AWS API Gateway and Azure API Management.
- **Chapter 6: Serverless Data Management Patterns**: Data management is a critical challenge in serverless architectures. This chapter covers how to manage state, storage, and data consistency in a serverless environment.
- **Chapter 7: Security Patterns for Serverless Architectures**: We focus on the security challenges in serverless and how to design secure systems using best practices like authentication, encryption, and API protection.
- **Chapter 8: Serverless Orchestration Patterns**: This chapter explores how to orchestrate complex workflows and processes using serverless technologies like AWS Step Functions and Azure Durable Functions.
- **Chapter 9: Hybrid Serverless Architectures**: Sometimes serverless needs to be combined with traditional infrastructures. This chapter covers when and how to use hybrid architectures effectively.
- **Chapter 10: Serverless CI/CD Pipelines and DevOps**: We delve into building continuous integration and continuous delivery pipelines for

serverless applications, automating deployments, and incorporating best practices from DevOps.

- **Chapter 11: Performance and Cost Optimization in Serverless**: Cost control and performance are crucial in serverless environments. This chapter provides techniques and tools for optimizing both.

- **Chapter 12: Patterns for Scaling Serverless Applications**: Scaling is one of serverless's strengths. This chapter looks at how to ensure your serverless applications can handle scaling challenges.

- **Chapter 13: Testing and Debugging Serverless Applications**: Testing serverless systems can be tricky. This chapter offers strategies for effectively testing and debugging serverless code.

- **Chapter 14: Future Trends in Serverless Architecture Patterns**: Serverless is an evolving space. We explore emerging trends and the future of serverless computing, including edge computing and AI workloads.

- **Conclusion: Mastering Serverless Architecture**: We wrap up by summarizing the key lessons, providing advice for continued learning, and sharing additional resources for deepening your serverless expertise.

Chapter 1: Understanding Serverless Computing Basics

What is Serverless Computing?

Serverless computing represents a new paradigm in cloud computing, where the need for developers to manage infrastructure is removed. Instead of provisioning and maintaining servers, developers write code and deploy it directly to a platform managed by a cloud provider. In this model, the cloud provider automatically handles the operational aspects like scaling, load balancing, and server maintenance.

Serverless computing allows teams to focus on business logic while relying on the provider for backend operations. The term "serverless" can be a bit misleading because servers are still involved, but their management is entirely abstracted away from the developer.

Advantages of Serverless Computing

1. **No Infrastructure Management**: The main attraction of serverless computing is that developers no longer need to worry about provisioning servers, managing capacity, or maintaining infrastructure.

2. **Scalability**: Serverless platforms scale applications automatically. Whether there's one user or a million, the application adapts to the demand without manual intervention.

3. **Cost Efficiency**: Serverless computing operates on a pay-as-you-go

model, meaning you only pay for the compute resources when your code is executing. This eliminates the cost of idle resources.

How It Differs from Traditional Architectures

- **Serverless**: Developers focus entirely on the code and its execution logic, leaving server provisioning, scaling, and maintenance to the cloud provider.
- **Traditional**: Requires developers or operations teams to manage hardware, operating systems, and network configurations. Even in virtualized cloud environments (IaaS), there's still a need for server setup and maintenance.

Serverless computing introduces more flexibility, agility, and cost efficiency, particularly in modern cloud-native environments where applications are increasingly dynamic and need to scale in response to varying demand.

The Serverless Ecosystem: AWS, Azure, Google Cloud

The serverless ecosystem is dominated by major cloud providers like AWS, Microsoft Azure, and Google Cloud, each offering unique serverless platforms and services. While their offerings are similar, there are distinctions in pricing models, feature sets, and integration with other cloud services.

Amazon Web Services (AWS)

AWS is a pioneer in the serverless space, with its introduction of AWS Lambda in 2014, which allows developers to run code in response to events without provisioning or managing servers. AWS offers a rich suite of complementary serverless services:

- **AWS Lambda**: Function-as-a-Service (FaaS) allowing developers to run code in response to events.
- **Amazon API Gateway**: A fully managed service to create, publish, and secure APIs.
- **Amazon DynamoDB**: A key-value and document-based database ideal for serverless architectures.

- **Amazon S3**: A storage service that integrates seamlessly with Lambda for event-driven functions.

Microsoft Azure

Microsoft Azure provides a competitive suite of serverless services with Azure Functions being its primary FaaS platform. Azure integrates its serverless offerings with other Microsoft services and products, making it a go-to platform for businesses already invested in the Microsoft ecosystem:

- **Azure Functions**: FaaS platform that allows code to be triggered by HTTP requests, timers, or events.
- **Azure Logic Apps**: Helps developers automate workflows and orchestrate various services.
- **Azure Event Grid**: A service that facilitates event routing and orchestration between Azure services and other platforms.
- **Azure Cosmos DB**: A globally distributed, multi-model database service that integrates with Azure Functions for scalable serverless applications.

Google Cloud

Google Cloud's serverless platform is driven by simplicity and ease of use. Google's serverless offerings integrate well with its extensive suite of machine learning and data analytics services:

- **Google Cloud Functions**: A FaaS platform similar to AWS Lambda, allowing developers to run code in response to events.
- **Google Cloud Run**: A managed compute platform that enables developers to run stateless containers without managing the underlying infrastructure.
- **Google Firebase**: A Backend-as-a-Service (BaaS) that provides a real-time database, authentication, and analytics for mobile and web applications.
- **Google Cloud Pub/Sub**: A fully managed messaging service that enables event-driven architectures.

Comparing the Ecosystems

While AWS is often seen as the most feature-rich, Azure's strong integration with enterprise tools (like Microsoft Active Directory and Office 365) makes it attractive to businesses that are already in the Microsoft ecosystem. Google Cloud, on the other hand, appeals to organizations focused on data analytics and machine learning due to its seamless integration with AI-driven tools.

Each provider offers robust solutions, but choosing the right one depends on your specific use case, pricing requirements, and existing infrastructure.

Core Components: Functions-as-a-Service (FaaS), Backend-as-a-Service (BaaS)

Serverless computing is built around two primary service models: Functions-as-a-Service (FaaS) and Backend-as-a-Service (BaaS). Each provides critical components that allow serverless applications to be developed, deployed, and managed efficiently.

Functions-as-a-Service (FaaS)

FaaS is the core of serverless computing. It allows developers to write individual pieces of code (functions) that execute in response to specific events, such as HTTP requests, file uploads, or database changes. FaaS abstracts away the complexity of server management, letting developers focus entirely on writing business logic.

How FaaS Works:

- Developers write code and deploy it to the cloud provider's FaaS platform.
- The cloud provider provisions and manages the necessary compute resources.
- Functions are executed in response to events and automatically scaled up or down based on demand.

Advantages of FaaS:

- **Event-Driven**: Functions are only executed when an event triggers them, making it ideal for sporadic workloads.
- **Scalability**: Functions scale automatically, allowing them to handle

unpredictable traffic.
- **Cost-Effective**: The pay-per-execution model ensures that you only pay for the resources when the function is actually running.

Backend-as-a-Service (BaaS)

BaaS is a set of cloud services that abstracts backend processes, allowing developers to focus on the frontend of an application. BaaS typically includes services like databases, authentication, cloud storage, and real-time communication.

Common BaaS Features:

- **Database Management**: Managed databases like Amazon DynamoDB, Google Firebase, or Azure Cosmos DB allow developers to store and retrieve data without worrying about scaling or provisioning.
- **Authentication**: Services like AWS Cognito, Firebase Authentication, and Azure Active Directory provide secure, scalable user authentication mechanisms.
- **Real-Time Communication**: Some BaaS platforms provide real-time data syncing, particularly useful in applications where real-time updates are critical (e.g., chat apps, live collaboration tools).

Advantages of BaaS:

- **Faster Development**: Since the backend is managed by the provider, developers can focus on frontend features and business logic.
- **Lower Operational Overhead**: BaaS removes the need for managing servers, databases, and other backend components.
- **Scalability**: Like FaaS, BaaS components scale automatically, which makes it easy to handle fluctuating workloads.

Both FaaS and BaaS work together to create a cohesive serverless architecture, with FaaS handling event-driven code execution and BaaS providing the backend services required to build complete applications.

Stateless and Event-Driven Computing

Serverless architectures rely heavily on the concepts of statelessness and event-driven computing, which shape how applications are designed and executed.

Stateless Computing

In traditional architectures, applications often rely on maintaining state (i.e., data) between function calls. For example, a user session on a website may store data that is accessible across multiple pages. However, in serverless computing, each function is stateless, meaning it doesn't retain any data between executions.

Why Stateless?:

- Statelessness enables functions to be more scalable and portable because they don't depend on specific instances or previous invocations.
- It allows for better fault tolerance. Since there's no reliance on local state, if one function instance fails, another can quickly take its place without data loss.

Managing State in Stateless Systems: In serverless systems, state is often stored externally in databases or managed state stores like Amazon DynamoDB, Azure Cosmos DB, or Google Cloud Datastore. By keeping the state separate from the application code, functions can remain lightweight and scalable.

Event-Driven Computing

Serverless functions are often triggered by events—this could be an API call, a database update, a file upload, or a scheduled task. This event-driven model is a key feature of serverless computing, allowing applications to react in real-time to changes in the system.

Event Sources:

- **HTTP Requests**: API calls via services like API Gateway.
- **Database Triggers**: Changes in databases triggering specific actions.
- **File Uploads**: Functions being invoked when files are uploaded to cloud

storage (e.g., Amazon S3).

- **Scheduled Jobs**: Functions that run based on a time-based trigger.

Advantages of Event-Driven Systems:

- **Real-Time Processing**: Event-driven architectures enable real-time response to user interactions, making them ideal for applications that require immediacy, like data processing, IoT, or user authentication.
- **Decoupled Services**: Functions can operate independently of each other, reducing dependencies and improving fault tolerance.

Together, stateless and event-driven computing form the foundation of modern serverless applications, allowing for better scalability, cost-efficiency, and simplicity in design.

When to Choose Serverless Over Traditional Architectures

Choosing between serverless and traditional architectures can depend on several factors, including the type of application, expected traffic, and long-term cost considerations.

When to Choose Serverless

- **Unpredictable Traffic**: Serverless is ideal for applications with unpredictable traffic patterns. Since the platform scales automatically, you don't have to worry about over-provisioning or under-provisioning resources.
- **Event-Driven Applications**: If your application is event-driven (e.g., a notification system, file processing, data pipeline), serverless can simplify the process by triggering functions only when events occur.
- **Cost Efficiency**: For applications with sporadic usage, serverless can be more cost-efficient than traditional setups, as you only pay for what you use. This makes it ideal for startups, small businesses, and proof-of-concept projects.

When Traditional Architectures are Better

- **Constant Workloads**: Applications with constant, predictable traffic may be better suited for traditional architectures, where you can reserve resources and achieve cost savings through long-term contracts or reserved instances.
- **Complex, Stateful Applications**: Applications that require maintaining complex state across sessions may struggle in serverless environments, especially if the external state store introduces latency.
- **Strict Performance Requirements**: In cases where performance and low latency are mission-critical, serverless may not be the best choice, particularly if cold starts are a concern.

Choosing between serverless and traditional architectures requires understanding the specific needs of your application and weighing the trade-offs. While serverless offers immense flexibility, scalability, and cost savings for certain use cases, it may not always be the right fit for every scenario.

This chapter serves as the foundation for understanding serverless computing. It introduces the core concepts, highlights the benefits and trade-offs, and provides insight into when serverless is the most appropriate choice for building modern applications.

Chapter 2: Introduction to Software Architecture Patterns

O verview of Architecture Patterns

In software engineering, architecture patterns provide a blueprint for structuring systems and solving recurring design challenges. These patterns serve as reusable solutions, tested and proven across various software development contexts. Architecture patterns are essential not only for large-scale systems but also for designing resilient, scalable, and maintainable systems across different environments—including serverless.

Serverless computing introduces a new realm of architectural considerations, shifting the focus from hardware management to application logic and cloud-managed services. Traditional architecture patterns such as monolithic, layered, and microservices need to be adapted to fit the serverless paradigm, which offers flexibility but comes with its own constraints. In a serverless environment, the architecture must accommodate the lack of long-running infrastructure and the stateless, event-driven nature of functions.

Why Patterns Matter in Serverless Architectures

1. **Improved Scalability**: Patterns help ensure that serverless functions and services scale efficiently, meeting unpredictable workloads without manual intervention.

2. **Reduced Complexity**: By following architectural patterns, developers can design serverless systems that are easier to understand and maintain.

3. **Resilience and Fault Tolerance**: Patterns allow serverless architectures to handle failure gracefully, ensuring that applications continue to operate even when parts of the system fail.

4. **Optimized Cost Management**: Since serverless pricing is based on execution time and resource consumption, well-designed patterns help minimize costs by reducing redundant executions and optimizing resource allocation.

5. **Decoupling**: Patterns encourage loose coupling between system components, allowing services to evolve independently, improving flexibility and enabling easier system updates or scaling.

Types of Architecture Patterns in Software

In traditional environments, software architecture patterns are typically classified into the following types:

- **Layered (N-Tier)**: The system is divided into multiple layers, each responsible for a different part of the application (e.g., user interface, business logic, data access). In serverless, this pattern is often adapted by splitting the application into functions that each represent a layer, with different microservices or APIs handling individual responsibilities.

- **Event-Driven**: This pattern revolves around the production, detection, and reaction to events. Serverless computing fits naturally into this pattern since functions are inherently event-driven, triggered by HTTP requests, database changes, file uploads, etc.

- **Microservices**: The application is divided into a collection of loosely coupled services, each focused on a specific domain or function. In serverless computing, microservices are typically represented by distinct functions or small groups of functions that handle specific tasks or business logic.

- **Monolithic**: In a monolithic architecture, all parts of the system are interconnected and interdependent. In serverless, although monolithic architectures are less common, some systems may begin this way before migrating to more modular or microservice-based patterns.

- **CQRS (Command Query Responsibility Segregation)**: In this pattern, the responsibilities for handling commands (write operations) and queries (read operations) are separated. This is particularly useful in serverless systems that need to optimize read-heavy workloads or manage complex business rules across distributed functions.

Serverless-Specific Patterns

While traditional architectural patterns can be adapted to fit serverless computing, several patterns are unique to the serverless paradigm:

- **Function Chaining**: In serverless, complex workflows can be modeled by chaining functions together, where the output of one function becomes the input for another. This can be implemented using AWS Step Functions, Azure Durable Functions, or Google Cloud Composer.
- **Event-Driven Microservices**: Serverless applications often rely heavily on event-driven microservices. Functions are executed in response to events, enabling a decoupled architecture that can scale independently of other services.
- **Backend for Frontend (BFF)**: In this pattern, separate backend services are built to serve the needs of specific frontends, such as mobile or web applications. Serverless functions can be tailored to handle requests from different clients, improving performance and maintainability.

By leveraging these patterns, serverless architectures can achieve the desired balance of scalability, resilience, and simplicity.

Understanding Design Principles in Serverless

Design principles are fundamental guidelines that ensure serverless applications are built in a way that maximizes the benefits of cloud-native features while mitigating risks such as vendor lock-in, performance bottlenecks, or runaway costs. Unlike traditional systems, serverless designs must account for the stateless nature of functions, event-driven triggers, and the unique pricing model that charges based on usage.

1. Single Responsibility Principle (SRP)

Each function in a serverless system should focus on a single task or responsibility. This principle aligns naturally with the design of serverless systems, where Functions-as-a-Service (FaaS) platforms like AWS Lambda or Azure Functions encourage lightweight, single-purpose functions.

- **Example**: In an e-commerce platform, instead of having one large function handle all aspects of order processing, there could be separate functions for payment processing, inventory checking, and email notifications. Each function has a clear, distinct responsibility.

2. Statelessness

Statelessness is a core requirement of serverless functions. Since serverless functions can be invoked, paused, and restarted on different machines, they must not rely on any local state. Any state that needs to be persisted should be stored in external systems like databases, object storage, or managed services such as AWS DynamoDB, Google Firebase, or Azure Cosmos DB.

- **Example**: A function that processes user requests should store session information in a distributed store rather than relying on server memory. This allows the function to be invoked multiple times, regardless of which instance is running.

3. Loose Coupling

Loose coupling refers to designing services or functions that have minimal dependencies on each other. In serverless, this principle is vital because the system needs to function reliably even when individual components are updated, scaled, or fail. Loose coupling allows for better fault tolerance, scalability, and flexibility.

- **Example**: In a serverless chat application, the message service and notification service should not rely on one another's availability. Messages can be queued in a message broker (like AWS SQS or Azure Queue Storage), ensuring that if the notification service goes down, messages are not lost.

4. Event-Driven Design

Serverless architectures thrive in event-driven environments, where actions trigger functions in response to specific events. These events could be API requests, database updates, or messages in a queue. Event-driven design ensures that serverless applications remain responsive and adaptable to changes in the system.

- **Example**: A serverless file-processing system where files uploaded to an S3 bucket trigger a Lambda function to process the files and store the results in a database. The file upload is the event that drives the entire process.

5. Resilience and Fault Tolerance

Serverless systems must be designed to handle failure gracefully. While serverless platforms automatically manage infrastructure reliability, applications need to account for potential issues like network failures, third-party service downtime, or intermittent glitches.

- **Best Practices**: Implementing retries, fallbacks, or circuit breakers can help ensure that serverless functions recover from failure without affecting user experience.

6. Security by Design

Security is a priority in serverless architectures, given the potential for functions to interact with multiple services, store sensitive data, and be exposed to the public internet. Security by design involves incorporating encryption, access controls, and monitoring from the very beginning.

- **Best Practices**: Implement least-privilege access controls, use secure storage for environment variables, and ensure all APIs and functions are authenticated.

7. Cost Efficiency

One of the most appealing features of serverless computing is its cost model, where users are charged based on actual usage. However, to optimize cost efficiency, serverless systems must be designed to minimize unnecessary executions and resource consumption.

- **Best Practices**: Optimize functions for cold starts by reducing initialization time, set appropriate memory allocation based on function needs, and minimize unnecessary API calls or external service invocations.

Common Serverless Architecture Scenarios

Serverless computing can be applied across a range of scenarios, each benefiting from its flexibility, scalability, and pay-per-use model. Understanding common use cases helps in identifying where serverless is most valuable, especially in designing scalable, efficient, and resilient architectures.

1. RESTful APIs

One of the most frequent applications of serverless is in building APIs. With API Gateway services (such as AWS API Gateway, Azure API Management, or Google Cloud Endpoints), developers can build robust RESTful APIs backed by serverless functions that handle requests and return responses dynamically.

- **Example**: An e-commerce application where users interact with an API to browse products, make purchases, and manage their accounts. Serverless functions handle all the backend logic, including retrieving product information from a database and processing payments.

2. Real-Time Data Processing

Serverless is ideal for processing real-time streams of data, whether from IoT devices, log files, or user interactions. Platforms like AWS Lambda, Google Cloud Functions, and Azure Functions can ingest and process data in real-time from services like AWS Kinesis, Google Pub/Sub, or Azure Event Hub.

- **Example**: A serverless system that processes IoT data from sensors in a factory. Each sensor sends data to a queue, which triggers a function to process and store the data in real-time, generating insights for engineers.

3. Web Applications

Serverless architectures are also used to build full-stack web applications. Static assets (HTML, CSS, JavaScript) can be served from object storage like AWS S3 or Google Cloud

1/2

4o

ChatGPT said:

ChatGPT

Storage, while serverless functions handle backend processing.

- **Example**: A social media application where users can post updates, comment, and like posts. The frontend is hosted on a static site, while backend operations for user authentication, database management, and notifications are handled by serverless functions.

4. Scheduled Tasks and Automation

Serverless functions are well-suited for handling scheduled tasks and cron jobs. Developers can schedule functions to run at specified intervals, automating tasks such as data backups, report generation, or email notifications.

- **Example**: A function that runs nightly to aggregate sales data from a database and send reports to management via email.

5. Chatbots and Voice Assistants

Serverless computing is a good fit for building chatbots and voice assistants, where functions can handle incoming messages, process user requests, and return responses dynamically.

- **Example**: A customer support chatbot that integrates with various messaging platforms, using serverless functions to handle inquiries, check order statuses, and provide responses based on user interactions.

The Role of Microservices in Serverless

Microservices architecture complements serverless computing, as both paradigms emphasize modularity, scalability, and resilience. In a microservices approach, applications are divided into smaller, independent services that communicate through well-defined APIs. This architecture is particularly well-suited for serverless environments due to the following reasons:

1. Decomposition of Services

Microservices allow developers to decompose applications into smaller, manageable services. Each service can be implemented as a serverless function, allowing for independent deployment and scaling based on the service's specific workload.

- **Example**: In an online retail application, different microservices could handle user authentication, inventory management, payment processing, and order fulfillment, with each service implemented as a separate serverless function.

2. Independent Scaling

One of the main advantages of serverless computing is its ability to scale individual functions independently based on demand. Microservices leverage this feature to ensure that services handling heavy loads can scale without affecting others.

- **Example**: During a sale event, the payment processing function may experience a spike in traffic while other services remain relatively stable.

Serverless allows the payment service to scale up automatically without impacting other services.

3. Technology Agnosticism

Microservices promote the use of diverse technologies and languages tailored to specific service needs. Serverless architectures align well with this philosophy, allowing developers to choose the best tools for each function or microservice without being constrained by a monolithic codebase.

- **Example**: A developer may implement the inventory management service in Node.js while the user authentication service is built in Python, allowing teams to leverage the strengths of each technology.

4. Enhanced Fault Isolation

In a microservices architecture, the failure of one service does not necessarily bring down the entire system. Serverless functions further enhance fault isolation since they can be designed to handle failures gracefully, utilizing patterns like retries, circuit breakers, and fallbacks.

- **Example**: If the order fulfillment service experiences downtime, users can still access the product catalog and make purchases, as the catalog service remains operational.

5. Continuous Deployment and Integration

Serverless microservices support continuous integration and deployment (CI/CD) practices, allowing developers to deploy updates independently and more frequently. This results in faster delivery of features and bug fixes.

- **Example**: An organization can adopt CI/CD pipelines that automatically deploy updates to individual serverless functions whenever code is pushed to the repository, minimizing downtime and accelerating development cycles.

Conclusion

In this chapter, we explored the foundational concepts of software architecture patterns, focusing on their importance in serverless computing. Understanding these patterns and design principles is crucial for developing scalable, resilient, and maintainable serverless applications.

We also examined common scenarios where serverless architectures thrive, showcasing the flexibility and advantages they bring. The integration of microservices with serverless computing further enhances application design, allowing teams to leverage the strengths of both paradigms.

As serverless computing continues to evolve, mastering architectural patterns will enable developers and architects to build effective and robust applications that can adapt to changing business needs and technology landscapes.

Chapter 3: Event-Driven Architectures

What is Event-Driven Architecture?

Event-driven architecture (EDA) is a software architectural pattern that promotes the production, detection, consumption, and reaction to events. In this model, events represent significant changes in state or actions that trigger subsequent processes. An event can be anything from a user action (like clicking a button) to system-generated signals (like database updates or timer-based triggers). EDA facilitates asynchronous communication between decoupled services, making it highly suitable for modern distributed systems, particularly in serverless computing.

Key Characteristics of Event-Driven Architecture

1. **Asynchronous Communication**: EDA allows different components of an application to communicate through events without requiring immediate responses, enabling greater flexibility and responsiveness.

2. **Loose Coupling**: In EDA, services are loosely coupled, meaning they do not directly depend on each other. This enhances system resilience; if one service fails, it does not impact others.

3. **Scalability**: EDA allows for natural scaling. As demand increases, event-driven systems can spin up multiple consumers to handle incoming events without significant architectural changes.

4. **Real-Time Processing**: Event-driven architectures are designed for handling real-time data, making them ideal for applications that require

immediate responses based on user actions or system changes.

5. **State Management**: EDA often relies on external state management solutions (like databases or caches) since events are generally stateless. This design encourages functions to react to events without retaining historical context.

Components of Event-Driven Architecture

- **Event Producers**: These are components that generate events. For example, a user uploading a photo to an application can trigger an event indicating a new photo is available for processing.
- **Event Channels**: This is the medium through which events are transmitted. Commonly used channels include message queues (like AWS SQS or RabbitMQ), event streams (like Apache Kafka or AWS Kinesis), and webhook notifications.
- **Event Consumers**: These components listen for events and perform actions based on the events received. In serverless architectures, event consumers are typically represented by serverless functions that are triggered when specific events occur.
- **Event Store**: An optional component, the event store records and retains events for future processing or auditing. This is useful for applications that need to maintain a history of events for analytics or replaying events.

Benefits of Event-Driven Architecture

1. **Improved Responsiveness**: EDA allows applications to respond to events in real-time, which is crucial for interactive applications or those requiring immediate feedback.
2. **Enhanced Flexibility**: By decoupling components, EDA enables developers to change or replace services without disrupting the entire system.
3. **Optimized Resource Utilization**: As event-driven systems scale dynamically based on incoming events, they help optimize resource

consumption, leading to cost savings, especially in serverless environments.

4. **Adaptability to Change**: EDA can quickly adapt to changing business requirements by allowing new event producers or consumers to be added without significant architectural changes.

5. **Streamlined Development**: Developers can work on different components independently, speeding up development cycles and enabling teams to adopt Agile methodologies more effectively.

Building Event-Driven Workflows with Serverless Functions

Serverless computing provides an ideal environment for implementing event-driven architectures. Functions-as-a-Service (FaaS) platforms like AWS Lambda, Azure Functions, and Google Cloud Functions are designed to respond to events, making it easier to build and deploy event-driven workflows.

Designing Event-Driven Workflows

1. **Identify Event Sources**: The first step in building an event-driven workflow is to identify the various sources of events that will trigger your functions. Common event sources include API Gateway requests, database changes (using triggers), file uploads to cloud storage, and messages from queues or streams.

2. **Define Event Types**: Once event sources are identified, you need to categorize the types of events that will trigger workflows. This could include user actions (like purchases or sign-ups), system events (like data updates), or scheduled tasks (like cron jobs).

3. **Create Event Producers**: For each identified event type, develop event producers that generate and publish events to the appropriate channels. For example, an e-commerce application could have a function that publishes an event to a message queue when a new order is placed.

4. **Build Event Consumers**: Create serverless functions that act as event consumers, listening for events from the channels you've defined. Each consumer should be responsible for handling a specific event type

and performing the necessary processing, such as updating databases, sending notifications, or triggering further workflows.

5. **Implement Event Routing**: Use message brokers or event routing services to manage the flow of events from producers to consumers. For example, AWS EventBridge can route events based on rules and conditions, directing them to the appropriate Lambda functions.

6. **Handle Errors and Retries**: Implement error handling and retry logic within your event consumers to ensure that events are processed reliably. For instance, if a function fails to process an event, it can be retried automatically, or the event can be routed to a dead-letter queue for later analysis.

7. **Monitor and Log Events**: Monitoring is crucial in event-driven systems. Use logging and monitoring tools to track event processing, detect bottlenecks, and analyze system performance. Services like AWS CloudWatch, Azure Monitor, and Google Stackdriver can help provide insights into your event-driven workflows.

Example: Building a Simple Event-Driven Workflow

Let's consider a practical example of an event-driven workflow in an e-commerce application:

1. **Event Source**: A user places an order through the website, triggering an API Gateway event.
2. **Event Producer**: The API Gateway publishes an "Order Placed" event to an AWS SNS (Simple Notification Service) topic.
3. **Event Routing**: AWS SNS routes the event to multiple subscribers, including:

- An AWS Lambda function that processes payments.
- Another Lambda function that updates inventory levels.
- A third function that sends confirmation emails to the user.

1. **Event Consumers**: Each Lambda function processes the event indepen-

dently. For example, the payment processing function checks payment details, and if successful, it publishes a "Payment Confirmed" event.

2. **Further Processing**: Other functions can be triggered by the "Payment Confirmed" event, such as a fulfillment service that prepares the order for shipping.

By following this workflow, the application can efficiently handle user orders in a responsive and scalable manner, taking full advantage of the serverless model.

Real-World Use Cases

Event-driven architectures find applications across various industries, thanks to their flexibility and ability to handle dynamic workloads. Below, we explore several real-world use cases, focusing on scenarios that benefit significantly from event-driven serverless systems.

1. Real-Time Data Processing

In industries where timely information is critical, such as finance or logistics, real-time data processing is paramount. Event-driven architectures allow organizations to process data as it arrives, enabling swift decision-making.

- **Example**: A stock trading platform utilizes event-driven architecture to process market data. When stock prices fluctuate, data is sent to a streaming service (like AWS Kinesis). This data triggers Lambda functions that analyze price trends, update user portfolios, and send alerts to investors in real-time.

2. Internet of Things (IoT)

The IoT landscape generates massive amounts of data from sensors and devices, making event-driven architectures ideal for handling incoming data streams and reacting to changes.

- **Example**: A smart home system utilizes IoT devices that send events when sensors detect changes, such as temperature fluctuations or security breaches. These events trigger serverless functions that adjust the thermostat, send notifications to homeowners, or log data for analytics.

3. User Interaction and Notification Systems

Applications that rely on user interactions, such as messaging or social media platforms, benefit from event-driven designs that provide real-time responses and notifications.

- **Example**: A messaging app that notifies users of new messages can implement an event-driven workflow. When a message is sent, an event is published, triggering a function that updates the recipient's notification status and sends a push notification to their device.

4. E-Commerce and Order Processing

Event-driven architectures can significantly improve the efficiency of e-commerce applications, where user actions lead to various downstream processes.

- **Example**: An e-commerce platform can implement event-driven work-flows to handle customer actions such as placing an order, adding items to a cart, or leaving a review. Each of these actions can trigger functions that process payments, manage inventory, and send order confirmation emails, ensuring a smooth customer experience.

5. Content Management Systems

For content-heavy applications, event-driven architectures help manage updates, content publication, and notifications efficiently.

- **Example**: A blogging platform can use an event-driven approach to handle new content submissions. When a new blog post is submitted, an event triggers functions that validate the submission, update the database, and notify subscribers about the new content.

Best Practices for Event-Driven Systems in Serverless

Implementing event-driven architectures in serverless environments offers numerous advantages, but it also requires careful consideration of best practices to ensure reliability, scalability, and maintainability.

1. Design for Failure

Assume that failures will occur and design your event-driven systems accordingly. Implement retries, dead-letter queues, and fallback mechanisms to handle errors gracefully. For example, if a Lambda function fails to process an event, configure a retry policy to re-at

4o mini

ChatGPT said:

ChatGPT

tempt processing a specific number of times before moving the event to a dead-letter queue for further analysis.

2. Use Idempotency

Ensure that your event consumers are idempotent, meaning they can process the same event multiple times without side effects. This is particularly important in distributed systems where events might be retried due to failures.

- **Example**: In a payment processing function, check if a payment has already been processed before attempting to execute the transaction again.

3. Keep Events Lightweight

Design events to be lightweight and focused. Include only the necessary information needed to process the event, as this minimizes overhead and improves performance.

- **Best Practice**: Use JSON to structure your event data and avoid sending large payloads unless absolutely necessary.

4. Monitor and Log Events

Implement robust monitoring and logging mechanisms to track event flow and performance. Use tools like AWS CloudWatch, Azure Monitor, or Google Cloud Operations Suite to gain visibility into event processing, detect anomalies, and optimize performance.

- **Best Practice**: Set up alerts for failures or high latency in event processing to quickly respond to issues.

5. Version Your Events

As your application evolves, so will the structure of your events. Implement versioning for your events to ensure backward compatibility and allow consumers to adapt to changes without disruption.

- **Example**: Include a version number in your event schema, allowing consumers to handle different versions of events gracefully.

6. Use Event Schema Validation

Implement schema validation to ensure that events conform to expected formats. This can help prevent errors caused by malformed events and improve data integrity.

- **Best Practice**: Utilize tools like JSON Schema or Protocol Buffers to define and validate your event structures.

7. Optimize for Cold Starts

In serverless architectures, cold starts can introduce latency when a function is invoked after being idle. Optimize functions by minimizing initialization time, keeping the function lightweight, and using provisioned concurrency if supported by your cloud provider.

- **Best Practice**: Pre-warm functions by invoking them periodically during low traffic to reduce cold start impacts.

Conclusion

Event-driven architectures represent a powerful paradigm for designing serverless applications, providing flexibility, scalability, and real-time responsiveness. By understanding the core concepts of EDA, developers can build effective workflows that respond to events in real time, enhancing user experiences and optimizing resource utilization.

This chapter has explored the foundations of event-driven architectures, delving into how serverless functions can be structured to create efficient, responsive systems. By examining real-world use cases and highlighting best practices, we have established a framework for successfully implementing event-driven systems in serverless environments.

As we continue our exploration of serverless computing, the next chapters will focus on more advanced topics, including the integration of serverless architectures with microservices and the complexities involved in managing distributed systems.

Chapter 4: Microservices in Serverless Computing

Microservices Architecture: The Serverless Approach

Microservices architecture has gained significant traction over the past decade due to its ability to enhance scalability, agility, and maintainability in software development. This architectural style structures an application as a collection of small, autonomous services, each focused on a specific business function. Microservices are designed to operate independently, allowing teams to deploy, scale, and manage them without affecting other parts of the application.

Serverless computing complements microservices by removing the overhead of infrastructure management, enabling developers to focus solely on writing code. With serverless, each microservice can be implemented as a serverless function (Function-as-a-Service), allowing for seamless scaling, reduced operational costs, and enhanced responsiveness to changing business needs.

Key Characteristics of Serverless Microservices

1. **Independence**: Each microservice can be developed, deployed, and scaled independently. This independence is crucial for teams working in parallel, as it enables them to innovate without waiting for other parts of the application.

2. **Event-Driven**: Serverless microservices often operate in an event-driven manner, reacting to events from various sources, such as API calls, message queues, or changes in data stores. This model allows for greater flexibility and responsiveness.

3. **Managed Infrastructure**: Serverless platforms automatically manage the infrastructure, including scaling and load balancing. Developers can focus on writing business logic rather than managing servers.

4. **Cost Efficiency**: With serverless microservices, you only pay for the resources consumed during execution. This pay-as-you-go model reduces costs, especially for workloads with variable usage patterns.

5. **Scalability**: Serverless platforms can automatically scale the number of function instances based on incoming traffic or events, ensuring optimal performance even under high loads.

Benefits of Combining Microservices with Serverless

- **Faster Time to Market**: By leveraging serverless, teams can rapidly develop and deploy microservices, leading to shorter development cycles and quicker delivery of features.
- **Enhanced Agility**: Teams can iterate and improve specific microservices without impacting the entire application, fostering a culture of continuous improvement and innovation.
- **Simplified Operations**: Serverless abstracts the complexities of infrastructure management, allowing teams to focus on developing and maintaining their services rather than worrying about servers and scaling.

Challenges of Serverless Microservices

Despite the benefits, there are challenges to consider when implementing serverless microservices:

- **Cold Start Latency**: Serverless functions may experience increased latency when they have not been invoked for a while. This cold start can impact user experience, particularly for latency-sensitive applications.

- **Vendor Lock-In**: Relying on a specific serverless provider can lead to vendor lock-in, making it difficult to migrate to another platform in the future.
- **Complexity in Monitoring and Debugging**: Debugging serverless microservices can be more complex due to their distributed nature and the statelessness of functions. Developers need to implement robust logging and monitoring to gain visibility into the system.

Overall, adopting microservices within a serverless architecture can lead to more efficient and scalable applications, provided that the challenges are addressed with appropriate strategies and tools.

Managing Dependencies and Service Interaction

One of the defining features of microservices architecture is the independence of services. However, this independence also introduces complexities related to managing dependencies and service interactions. In serverless microservices, understanding how services communicate and depend on each other is critical for building robust applications.

Understanding Dependencies in Microservices

Dependencies in microservices refer to the relationships between different services that require interaction to perform a task. These dependencies can be classified into two main categories:

1. **Synchronous Dependencies**: When a service makes a direct call to another service and waits for a response, it creates a synchronous dependency. For example, a user authentication service may need to verify user credentials against a user database before allowing access to other services.
2. **Asynchronous Dependencies**: In this model, services communicate through events or messages without waiting for immediate responses. This decouples services and allows them to operate independently. An example of this would be a payment processing service that publishes an event to a message queue after completing a transaction, allowing other services to react to that event asynchronously.

Challenges of Managing Dependencies

- **Tight Coupling**: Synchronous dependencies can lead to tight coupling between services, where one service's availability directly impacts another's. This can introduce failure points and reduce the overall resilience of the system.
- **Latency Issues**: Synchronous calls can introduce latency, affecting the user experience. If one service takes too long to respond, it can slow down the entire request-response cycle.
- **Monitoring Complexity**: As the number of services increases, monitoring and debugging dependencies can become increasingly complex. Understanding the flow of data and events between services requires robust logging and tracing mechanisms.

Best Practices for Managing Dependencies

1. **Favor Asynchronous Communication**: Whenever possible, use asynchronous communication methods (like message queues or event streams) to reduce tight coupling and improve scalability. This allows services to process events independently and reduces the risk of cascading failures.
2. **Implement Circuit Breakers**: To protect against failures, implement circuit breakers that prevent a service from making calls to a dependent service that is known to be failing. This allows the system to recover gracefully without overwhelming the failing service.
3. **Use Service Discovery**: In a microservices architecture, using a service discovery mechanism can help manage dependencies dynamically. Service discovery enables services to find and communicate with each other without hardcoding endpoints, improving flexibility.
4. **Maintain Clear Interfaces**: Define clear and well-documented APIs for each service. This ensures that changes to one service do not disrupt others and makes it easier to manage dependencies.
5. **Monitor and Trace Interactions**: Implement comprehensive moni-

toring and tracing to track the flow of requests and responses between services. Tools like AWS X-Ray, Azure Monitor, and OpenTelemetry can provide visibility into service interactions and help identify bottlenecks or failures.

Implementing Microservices with AWS Lambda, Azure Functions, and Google Cloud Functions

AWS Lambda, Azure Functions, and Google Cloud Functions are the leading platforms for implementing serverless microservices. Each platform offers unique features and capabilities that developers can leverage to build scalable and resilient microservices.

Implementing Microservices with AWS Lambda

AWS Lambda allows developers to run code without provisioning or managing servers. Lambda supports various programming languages and integrates seamlessly with other AWS services.

- **Creating a Lambda Function**: Developers can create a Lambda function using the AWS Management Console, AWS CLI, or infrastructure-as-code tools like AWS CloudFormation or AWS SAM (Serverless Application Model).
- **Event Sources**: AWS Lambda can be triggered by multiple event sources, including API Gateway, DynamoDB Streams, S3 events, and SNS notifications. This flexibility allows for various event-driven workflows.
- **Managing Dependencies**: Developers can package dependencies within the Lambda deployment package or use Lambda layers to manage shared libraries efficiently.

Example: Building an E-Commerce Microservice with AWS Lambda

1. **User Service**: A Lambda function manages user registrations and logins, interacting with an Amazon DynamoDB table for user data storage.
2. **Product Service**: Another Lambda function handles product catalog management, fetching product information from a separate DynamoDB

table.

3. **Order Service**: The order processing Lambda function receives events from API Gateway when a user places an order. It interacts with both the User and Product services to validate the order and update inventory.

Each service can be deployed independently, allowing for continuous deployment and updates without downtime.

Implementing Microservices with Azure Functions

Azure Functions offers a similar serverless experience, allowing developers to build event-driven applications with integrated tools and services in the Microsoft Azure ecosystem.

- **Function Triggers and Bindings**: Azure Functions supports various triggers (HTTP requests, timers, queues) and bindings (input and output), simplifying the integration with Azure services like Azure Cosmos DB, Azure Blob Storage, and Azure Event Grid.
- **Local Development**: Developers can use the Azure Functions Core Tools to develop and test functions locally before deploying them to Azure.

Example: Building a Chat Application with Azure Functions

1. **Message Service**: An Azure Function processes incoming messages from users, storing them in Azure Cosmos DB.
2. **Notification Service**: Another function sends notifications to users when they receive new messages, using Azure Notification Hubs for push notifications.
3. **User Management**: A separate function handles user authentication and profile management, interacting with Azure Active Directory for user identity management.

Implementing Microservices with Google Cloud Functions

Google Cloud Functions allows developers to create single-purpose functions that respond to events from Google Cloud services, making it easy to build microservices within the Google Cloud ecosystem.

- **Event-Driven Architecture**: Google Cloud Functions can be triggered by a variety of events, including HTTP requests, Pub/Sub messages, and changes in Cloud Storage or Firestore.
- **Integration with Other Google Services**: The integration with other Google services simplifies data management, real-time analytics, and machine learning applications.

Example: Building a File Processing Service with Google Cloud Functions

1. **Upload Function**: A Cloud Function is triggered when a user uploads a file to Google Cloud Storage. It processes the file (e.g., image resizing or format conversion) and saves the results in another storage bucket.
2. **Notification Function**: After processing, another function sends a notification to users via email or messaging services, informing them of the completed task.
3. **Analytics Function**: A separate function can log file processing events to Google BigQuery for real-time analytics and reporting.

Handling Communication Between Serverless Microservices

In a microservices architecture, effective communication between services is essential for ensuring the overall functionality and performance of the application. In serverless environments, communication can occur through various mechanisms, each with its own strengths and trade-offs.

1. Synchronous Communication

Synchronous communication involves direct calls between services where one service waits for a response from another. This model is common in microservices but can lead to tight coupling and latency issues if not managed properly.

- **Example**: A user service may call a payment service to process transactions. The user service waits for the payment service to respond before proceeding. While this approach is straightforward, it can introduce latency and bottlenecks, particularly if the payment service experiences delays.

2. Asynchronous Communication

Asynchronous communication allows services to interact without waiting for immediate responses, reducing coupling and improving responsiveness. In serverless architectures, asynchronous communication is typically implemented using message queues or event streams.

- **Message Queues**: Services can send messages to a queue (like AWS SQS or Azure Queue Storage) that other services consume. This decouples the services and allows them to operate independently.
- **Event Streams**: Event streaming platforms (like Apache Kafka or AWS Kinesis) enable services to publish events to a stream, where other services can subscribe and react to those events in real-time.

3. API Gateways

API gateways provide a unified entry point for microservices, handling routing, authentication, and other cross-cutting concerns. They simplify the interaction between services and enable developers to manage APIs efficiently.

- **Example**: An API Gateway can route requests from clients to different serverless functions based on the URL path, allowing for organized access to microservices without exposing the underlying architecture to clients.

4. Service Mesh

A service mesh provides a dedicated infrastructure layer for managing service-to-service communication. It handles routing, load balancing, and observability, allowing developers to focus on application logic.

- **Example**: Using a service mesh like Istio or Linkerd can provide advanced features such as traffic management, security policies, and detailed telemetry, which can enhance the resilience and observability of serverless microservices.

Conclusion

In this chapter, we explored the integration of microservices within serverless computing, highlighting the advantages, challenges, and best practices. Microservices architecture, when combined with serverless computing, allows organizations to build scalable, resilient applications that can rapidly respond to changing business needs.

We examined how to implement microservices using leading serverless platforms like AWS Lambda, Azure Functions, and Google Cloud Functions, focusing on building independent services that communicate effectively. Finally, we discussed the various communication methods available for serverless microservices, emphasizing the importance of choosing the right approach to ensure optimal performance and reliability.

As we continue our exploration of serverless architectures, the next chapters will delve deeper into specific implementation strategies, security considerations, and advanced architectural patterns that enhance the effectiveness of serverless microservices in modern applications.

Chapter 5: API Gateway Design Patterns

Introduction to API Gateways in Serverless Architectures

In the realm of modern software development, APIs (Application Programming Interfaces) play a critical role in enabling communication between different systems. As applications increasingly adopt microservices and serverless architectures, API Gateways have emerged as a crucial component that helps manage these interactions. An API Gateway acts as a single entry point for clients, handling requests and routing them to the appropriate microservices or serverless functions.

API Gateways streamline the process of exposing microservices and serverless functions to clients, providing a host of features that enhance security, performance, and manageability. They serve as intermediaries, enabling developers to enforce policies, monitor traffic, and optimize resource usage.

In this chapter, we will delve into the design patterns associated with API Gateways in serverless architectures. We will explore the key features and benefits of using API Gateways, discuss various design patterns, and provide guidance on implementing and managing API Gateways effectively.

The Role of API Gateways

API Gateways serve multiple purposes in serverless architectures, including:

1. **Request Routing**: API Gateways route incoming requests from clients to the appropriate serverless functions or microservices based on predefined rules.

2. **Authentication and Authorization**: API Gateways can enforce security measures by handling authentication and authorization, ensuring that only authorized clients can access certain resources.

3. **Rate Limiting and Throttling**: To protect backend services from being overwhelmed by excessive traffic, API Gateways can implement rate limiting and throttling policies.

4. **Caching**: API Gateways can cache responses to reduce the load on backend services and improve response times for frequently accessed data.

5. **Monitoring and Analytics**: API Gateways provide built-in monitoring and analytics features that enable developers to track API usage, identify bottlenecks, and gain insights into application performance.

6. **Error Handling**: API Gateways can manage error responses and provide standardized error messages, improving the overall user experience.

7. **Transformation and Aggregation**: API Gateways can transform requests and responses, allowing for data formatting changes or aggregating responses from multiple microservices into a single response.

API Gateway Design Patterns

Design patterns for API Gateways are critical for effectively managing and optimizing the interactions between clients and serverless functions or microservices. Below are several commonly used API Gateway design patterns in serverless architectures.

1. Basic Routing Pattern

The Basic Routing Pattern is the foundation of API Gateways. It involves directing incoming API requests to the corresponding backend services based on the request path or HTTP method.

- **How It Works**: When a client sends a request to the API Gateway, the Gateway examines the request and routes it to the appropriate serverless function or microservice based on predefined rules.

- **Use Case**: This pattern is ideal for straightforward applications where each endpoint corresponds directly to a serverless function. For example, an e-commerce application might have endpoints for user registration, product listings, and order processing, each mapped to their respective Lambda functions.

2. Proxy Pattern

The Proxy Pattern is an extension of the Basic Routing Pattern that acts as a direct proxy between the client and the backend services. The API Gateway forwards requests and responses without altering them.

- **How It Works**: The API Gateway receives a request and forwards it to the appropriate service without modification. The response from the service is then sent back to the client.
- **Use Case**: This pattern is beneficial when you want to expose existing microservices without significant changes. For example, if you have an existing RESTful API, you can use an API Gateway as a proxy to manage authentication, logging, and monitoring without modifying the backend services.

3. Aggregation Pattern

The Aggregation Pattern allows the API Gateway to consolidate responses from multiple microservices into a single response. This is particularly useful in scenarios where clients require data from various services to fulfill a single request.

- **How It Works**: The API Gateway receives a request and calls multiple backend services concurrently. It then aggregates the responses and sends a unified response back to the client.
- **Use Case**: In a social media application, a user profile page might require data from multiple services, such as user information, friends list, and recent posts. The API Gateway can aggregate this data from different

microservices and return it in a single API response.

4. Caching Pattern

The Caching Pattern enhances performance and reduces latency by storing frequently accessed data in the API Gateway. When a request is made for cached data, the Gateway can return the cached response without invoking the backend service.

- **How It Works**: The API Gateway checks if a cached response exists for the incoming request. If it does, the cached response is returned; otherwise, the request is forwarded to the backend service, and the response is cached for future use.
- **Use Case**: This pattern is beneficial for applications with read-heavy workloads or frequently accessed data, such as product information in an e-commerce application. Caching responses can significantly improve response times and reduce the load on backend services.

5. Transformation Pattern

The Transformation Pattern involves modifying requests and responses as they pass through the API Gateway. This can include changing data formats, adding or removing fields, or transforming data structures.

- **How It Works**: The API Gateway inspects incoming requests and applies transformation rules before forwarding them to the backend service. Similarly, responses from the backend can be transformed before sending them to the client.
- **Use Case**: This pattern is useful when integrating with third-party APIs or services that expect specific data formats. For example, if a client sends data in XML format but the backend service expects JSON, the API Gateway can convert the request format before routing it.

6. Security Pattern

The Security Pattern focuses on implementing security measures at the API

Gateway level. This includes authentication, authorization, and protection against common security threats such as DDoS attacks.

- **How It Works**: The API Gateway can enforce security policies, such as requiring API keys, validating JWT tokens, and implementing rate limiting to prevent abuse.
- **Use Case**: This pattern is critical for applications handling sensitive data, such as financial or personal information. Implementing security measures at the API Gateway helps protect backend services and ensures compliance with regulations.

7. Service Discovery Pattern

The Service Discovery Pattern allows the API Gateway to dynamically discover and route requests to backend services without hardcoding their addresses. This is particularly useful in microservices architectures where services may scale or change frequently.

- **How It Works**: The API Gateway queries a service registry (like AWS Service Discovery or Consul) to determine the available instances of a service and routes requests accordingly.
- **Use Case**: This pattern is beneficial in environments with frequent service scaling, as it allows the API Gateway to always route requests to the most up-to-date service instances.

Implementing API Gateways in Serverless Architectures

Implementing an API Gateway in serverless architectures involves several steps, from selecting the right platform to defining the gateway's configuration. Below, we outline the key steps for implementing API Gateways using AWS API Gateway, Azure API Management, and Google Cloud Endpoints.

1. Implementing AWS API Gateway

AWS API Gateway is a fully managed service that makes it easy to create, publish, maintain, and secure APIs at any scale. It integrates seamlessly with AWS Lambda and other AWS services.

Key Steps:

- **Create an API**: Use the AWS Management Console, AWS CLI, or AWS SAM to create a new API. Choose between REST API or HTTP API based on your requirements.
- **Define Resources and Methods**: Set up resources (e.g., /users, /products) and define the HTTP methods (GET, POST, PUT, DELETE) for each resource.
- **Integrate with AWS Lambda**: For each method, configure the integration to point to the appropriate AWS Lambda function that handles the request.
- **Configure Security**: Implement security measures, such as API keys, IAM roles, and resource policies to control access to your API.
- **Deploy the API**: Deploy the API to a stage (e.g., development, production) and provide a URL for clients to access it.
- **Monitoring and Logging**: Enable CloudWatch logging to monitor API usage, performance, and error rates.

Example Implementation:

For an e-commerce application, create an API in AWS API Gateway with resources for user management, product listings, and order processing. Each resource integrates with its respective Lambda function, and security is enforced using API keys and IAM roles.

2. Implementing Azure API Management

Azure API Management is a fully managed service that allows you to create, publish, secure, and analyze APIs in the Microsoft Azure ecosystem.

Key Steps:

- **Create an API Management Service**: Use the Azure Portal to create a new API Management instance.
- **Import or Define APIs**: You can import existing APIs or define new ones using the Azure portal or OpenAPI specifications.
- **Configure Policies**: Azure API Management allows you to configure

policies for request and response transformations, security, caching, and logging.

- **Integrate with Azure Functions**: For serverless applications, define operations that link to Azure Functions, specifying the HTTP methods and routes.
- **Publish and Monitor**: Once the APIs are configured, publish them to the developer portal, and use Azure Monitor to track usage, performance, and errors.

Example Implementation:

For a chat application, create an API in Azure API Management that connects to Azure Functions handling message processing, user authentication, and notifications. Use policies to transform request payloads and implement rate limiting.

3. Implementing Google Cloud Endpoints

Google Cloud Endpoints is a serverless API management system that provides a robust way to create, deploy, and manage APIs in the Google Cloud ecosystem.

Key Steps:

- **Define an OpenAPI Specification**: Create an OpenAPI specification that defines your API endpoints, methods, and authentication requirements.
- **Deploy the API**: Use Google Cloud Console or gcloud command-line tool to deploy the API configuration to Google Cloud Endpoints.
- **Integrate with Cloud Functions**: Link API methods to Google Cloud Functions to handle incoming requests.
- **Set Up Security**: Implement authentication using Firebase Authentication, Google Identity Platform, or API keys to secure your API.
- **Monitor and Log**: Utilize Google Cloud Monitoring and Logging to track API usage, performance metrics, and error rates.

Example Implementation:

For a real-time data processing application, use Google Cloud Endpoints to define an API that connects to Cloud Functions responsible for processing data streams. Implement security measures and monitor performance through integrated tools.

Handling Communication Between Serverless Microservices

Effective communication between serverless microservices is essential for building responsive and resilient applications. In this section, we will explore various communication methods, patterns, and best practices for enabling seamless interactions between serverless functions.

1. Synchronous Communication Methods

Synchronous communication methods involve direct calls between microservices, where one service waits for a response from another. While this approach can simplify interactions, it can also introduce latency and tight coupling.

Common Synchronous Communication Methods:

- **HTTP/REST Calls**: Using HTTP requests to communicate between services is the most straightforward method. For example, a user service may call a product service to retrieve product details.
- **GraphQL**: An alternative to REST, GraphQL allows clients to request only the data they need, reducing the number of requests required to gather related data.

Considerations:

- Ensure proper error handling and timeout mechanisms are in place to avoid prolonged waits in case of failures.
- Monitor and optimize performance, as synchronous calls can introduce latency, impacting the overall user experience.

2. Asynchronous Communication Methods

Asynchronous communication methods decouple services, allowing them to communicate through events or messages without waiting for immediate responses. This approach enhances scalability and resilience.

Common Asynchronous Communication Methods:

- **Message Queues**: Services communicate through message queues (e.g., AWS SQS, Azure Queue Storage), where producers send messages, and consumers process them independently.
- **Event Streams**: Event streaming platforms (e.g., AWS Kinesis, Apache Kafka) allow services to publish and consume events in real-time, enabling reactive architectures.

Considerations:

- Implement robust error handling and retry mechanisms to ensure that messages are processed reliably.
- Use idempotent consumers to handle duplicate messages gracefully.

3. Event-Driven Patterns for Communication

Leveraging event-driven patterns can enhance communication between serverless microservices, enabling more flexible and responsive architectures.

Common Event-Driven Patterns:

- **Publish-Subscribe**: In this pattern, services publish events to a message broker or event bus, and multiple subscribers listen for those events. This allows multiple services to react to the same event independently.
- **Fan-Out and Fan-In**: The Fan-Out pattern involves a single event triggering multiple services, while the Fan-In pattern aggregates responses from multiple services into a single result.

Considerations:

- Design events to be self-descriptive, allowing consumers to understand the context without requiring extensive documentation.
- Implement proper versioning for events to manage changes and ensure

backward compatibility.

Conclusion

In this chapter, we explored the integration of microservices within serverless computing, focusing on the role of API Gateways and the various design patterns associated with them. We examined how API Gateways streamline the process of managing microservices, providing essential features such as request routing, authentication, caching, and monitoring.

We also delved into the implementation of API Gateways using leading serverless platforms like AWS API Gateway, Azure API Management, and Google Cloud Endpoints, providing guidance on how to set up and manage APIs effectively.

Finally, we discussed the critical aspect of communication between serverless microservices, highlighting synchronous and asynchronous communication methods, event-driven patterns, and best practices for ensuring seamless interactions.

As we move forward in this book, the next chapters will focus on advanced topics in serverless computing, including security considerations, performance optimization, and real-world case studies that illustrate best practices in serverless architecture.

Chapter 6: Serverless Data Management Patterns

I ntroduction to Data Management in Serverless Architectures

Data management in serverless computing presents unique challenges and opportunities. Traditional architectures typically involve long-running applications that maintain state across sessions, often relying on relational databases and local storage. In contrast, serverless architectures embrace a stateless model where functions execute in response to events, requiring different approaches to data management.

In serverless environments, data is often distributed across various services and storage solutions. This distribution enables flexibility and scalability but introduces complexities related to state management, consistency, and performance. Understanding the data management patterns specific to serverless is crucial for building efficient, responsive applications.

This chapter explores the core concepts of data management in serverless architectures, including common patterns, challenges, and best practices for handling data in a serverless context.

Understanding the Challenges of Data Management in Serverless

Serverless computing introduces several challenges when it comes to data management:

1. **Statelessness**: Functions in serverless architectures are stateless, meaning they cannot retain information between invocations. This requires external storage solutions to manage state, making data access and retrieval crucial for maintaining application functionality.

2. **Cold Starts**: When a serverless function is invoked after a period of inactivity, it may experience a "cold start," where the initialization process adds latency. This is particularly significant when functions need to access external data stores, as the cold start can lead to slower response times.

3. **Eventual Consistency**: In a distributed environment, achieving strong consistency can be challenging. As functions may read and write to multiple data sources, managing eventual consistency becomes essential to ensure that all parts of the system reflect the most recent data.

4. **Data Latency**: Accessing data from external storage solutions introduces latency, which can impact the overall performance of serverless applications. The choice of data storage technology and its proximity to the executing function are critical factors in minimizing latency.

5. **Complexity of Data Management**: The need to manage data across various services and storage solutions can increase complexity. This complexity necessitates clear strategies for data access, transformation, and persistence.

Common Data Management Patterns in Serverless

To effectively manage data in serverless architectures, several data management patterns can be employed. Each pattern addresses specific challenges and provides solutions for efficient data handling.

1. Event Sourcing Pattern

Event sourcing is a pattern where the state of an application is determined by a sequence of events. Instead of storing the current state of the data directly, the application records each change as an event, enabling the reconstruction of the current state at any point in time.

- **How It Works**: When a change occurs (e.g., a user updates their profile), an event is created and stored in an event store (e.g., AWS DynamoDB, Kafka). The current state can be derived by replaying the events.

- **Benefits**:
- **Auditability**: Since all changes are recorded as events, it's easy to track the history of changes.
- **Decoupling**: Event sourcing decouples the write and read models, allowing different services to consume events independently.
- **Challenges**:
- **Event Schema Evolution**: As the application evolves, managing the schema of events can become complex.
- **Performance**: Replaying events to reconstruct state may introduce latency, particularly with a large number of events.

2. Command Query Responsibility Segregation (CQRS)

CQRS is a pattern that separates the responsibilities of reading and writing data. In serverless architectures, this separation allows for more optimized data access and can help address the challenges of scalability and complexity.

- **How It Works**: The application is divided into two parts: commands (which change state) and queries (which read data). Each part can be implemented independently, with different storage solutions optimized for their specific tasks.
- **Benefits**:
- **Optimized Performance**: Different data stores can be used for read and write operations, improving performance.
- **Scalability**: Each part can scale independently based on its workload, allowing for efficient resource allocation.
- **Challenges**:
- **Complexity**: Implementing CQRS requires careful planning and management of command and query models.
- **Eventual Consistency**: Since writes and reads are separated, ensuring consistency between the two can be challenging.

3. Stateless Data Management Pattern

In serverless architectures, the stateless nature of functions necessitates externalizing state management. The Stateless Data Management Pattern involves leveraging external data stores to maintain state while ensuring that functions remain stateless.

- **How It Works**: Functions access external data stores (like DynamoDB, Azure Cosmos DB, or Google Firestore) to read and write stateful information. This allows the function to execute without retaining local state.
- **Benefits**:
- **Simplicity**: Functions remain lightweight and focused on business logic without managing local state.
- **Scalability**: External data stores can scale independently of the functions, allowing for better performance under load.
- **Challenges**:
- **Latency**: Accessing external data stores can introduce latency, affecting the overall performance of serverless applications.
- **Transaction Management**: Managing transactions across stateless functions can be complex, especially when multiple functions need to operate on the same data.

4. Data Partitioning Pattern

Data partitioning involves dividing large datasets into smaller, more manageable parts to improve performance and scalability. This pattern is particularly useful in serverless architectures, where functions may operate on specific segments of data.

- **How It Works**: Datasets are partitioned based on a key (e.g., user ID, geographical region), allowing functions to process only the relevant partitions. This reduces the amount of data each function needs to access, improving performance.
- **Benefits**:

- **Performance**: By reducing the amount of data processed by each function, partitioning can lead to faster execution times.
- **Scalability**: Functions can scale independently based on the workload of each data partition.
- **Challenges**:
- **Complexity**: Implementing data partitioning requires careful design and management of partitions.
- **Data Retrieval**: Querying partitioned data may require more complex logic to ensure that all relevant partitions are accessed.

5. Caching Pattern

Caching is a widely used data management pattern that stores frequently accessed data in memory to improve performance. In serverless architectures, caching can significantly reduce latency and improve response times.

- **How It Works**: Cached data is stored in an in-memory data store (like AWS ElastiCache or Azure Redis Cache). When a function needs to access data, it first checks the cache before querying the primary data store.
- **Benefits**:
- **Reduced Latency**: Accessing data from memory is faster than querying a database, leading to improved response times.
- **Lower Load on Databases**: Caching reduces the number of read requests sent to the primary data store, improving overall performance.
- **Challenges**:
- **Cache Invalidation**: Managing the freshness of cached data can be complex. If the underlying data changes, the cache must be invalidated or updated accordingly.
- **Increased Complexity**: Implementing caching adds another layer of complexity to the application architecture.

Best Practices for Data Management in Serverless

To effectively manage data in serverless architectures, developers should adhere to best practices that optimize performance, ensure reliability, and enhance maintainability.

1. Choose the Right Data Storage Solutions

Selecting the appropriate data storage solution is critical for effective data management. Different storage technologies are suited for different use cases:

- **NoSQL Databases**: These are ideal for unstructured data or rapidly changing schemas, making them a good fit for serverless applications (e.g., AWS DynamoDB, MongoDB).
- **SQL Databases**: For applications requiring complex queries or transactions, relational databases may be more appropriate (e.g., Amazon RDS, Azure SQL Database).
- **Object Storage**: For storing large files or binary data, consider object storage solutions (e.g., AWS S3, Google Cloud Storage).

2. Optimize Data Access Patterns

Design your data access patterns to minimize latency and reduce the number of calls to external services. Consider using the following strategies:

- **Batch Processing**: When possible, batch multiple read or write operations into a single request to reduce the number of network calls.
- **Use Projections**: When implementing patterns like CQRS, create specialized views or projections of your data that are optimized for specific queries.

3. Implement Effective Caching Strategies

Use caching judiciously to improve performance and reduce load on data stores:

- **Cache Frequently Accessed Data**: Identify the most frequently accessed data and store it in an in-memory cache for rapid access.
- **Set Appropriate Cache Expiration**: Use expiration policies to ensure that cached data remains fresh and does not become stale.

4. Ensure Data Consistency

Maintaining data consistency across microservices and serverless functions is crucial, especially in distributed architectures:

- **Use Distributed Transactions**: For operations that span multiple services, consider using distributed transaction protocols or patterns like the Saga pattern to ensure consistency.
- **Implement Idempotency**: Ensure that operations are idempotent, allowing them to be retried without adverse effects if they fail.

5. Monitor Data Performance

Implement monitoring and logging to track data access patterns, performance metrics, and potential issues:

- **Use Monitoring Tools**: Leverage monitoring tools like AWS Cloud-Watch, Azure Monitor, or Google Cloud Monitoring to gain insights into data access and performance.
- **Analyze Usage Patterns**: Regularly analyze data access patterns to identify opportunities for optimization or re-architecture.

Conclusion

In this chapter, we explored the complexities and patterns associated with data management in serverless architectures. We examined common challenges, including statelessness, cold starts, eventual consistency, and data latency. Through various data management patterns—such as event sourcing, CQRS, stateless data management, data partitioning, and caching—we outlined strategies for effectively handling data in serverless environments.

Additionally, we discussed best practices for data management, emphasizing the importance of choosing the right storage solutions, optimizing data access patterns, implementing caching strategies, ensuring data consistency, and monitoring performance.

As we continue our journey through serverless computing, the next chapters will focus on advanced topics such as security considerations, performance optimization strategies, and real-world case studies that demonstrate best practices in serverless data management.

Chapter 7: Security Considerations in Serverless Computing

Introduction to Security in Serverless Architectures

As organizations increasingly adopt serverless computing, the security of applications deployed in this environment becomes paramount. Serverless architectures offer numerous benefits, such as reduced operational overhead, enhanced scalability, and cost efficiency. However, they also introduce unique security challenges that must be addressed to protect sensitive data and maintain the integrity of applications.

In traditional architectures, security responsibilities are often shared between the cloud provider and the organization. However, in serverless environments, this shared responsibility model shifts, placing more emphasis on the developer and the application owner to ensure security. Developers must understand the intricacies of securing serverless applications and implement strategies to mitigate risks.

This chapter explores the critical aspects of security in serverless computing, including the challenges posed by serverless architectures, strategies for securing serverless applications, and best practices for maintaining a secure environment.

Understanding Security Challenges in Serverless Architectures

Serverless architectures come with distinct security challenges that differ from traditional models. Understanding these challenges is the first step toward implementing effective security measures.

1. Shared Responsibility Model

In serverless computing, the responsibility for security is divided between the cloud provider and the user. While cloud providers are responsible for securing the underlying infrastructure, users are responsible for securing their applications and data.

- **User Responsibilities**: This includes managing access controls, securing API endpoints, and ensuring that serverless functions are designed with security in mind.
- **Provider Responsibilities**: Providers ensure that the infrastructure is protected against threats, maintain physical security, and keep the platform up to date with the latest security patches.

2. Increased Attack Surface

Serverless applications often consist of multiple functions, each exposed as an API endpoint. This increases the attack surface, as each endpoint can potentially be targeted by malicious actors.

- **API Security**: Exposed APIs must be secured to prevent unauthorized access and exploitation. Inadequate API security can lead to data breaches, denial-of-service attacks, and other security incidents.

3. Lack of Visibility and Control

Serverless architectures abstract away much of the underlying infrastructure, making it challenging to gain visibility into what is happening within the application.

- **Monitoring and Logging**: Traditional monitoring tools may not be sufficient for serverless environments. Developers need to implement effective logging and monitoring strategies to gain insights into function execution and detect anomalies.

4. Function-Level Security

Each serverless function is an independent unit of execution, which can lead to inconsistent security practices across functions. Developers may inadvertently introduce vulnerabilities if they do not follow security best practices for each function.

- **Inconsistent Configuration**: Functions may be deployed with varying security configurations, leading to potential security gaps.

5. Third-Party Dependencies

Serverless applications often rely on third-party libraries and services, which can introduce security risks. Vulnerabilities in these dependencies can expose the application to attacks.

- **Dependency Management**: Keeping third-party libraries up to date and ensuring that they are free from known vulnerabilities is critical for maintaining security.

Strategies for Securing Serverless Applications

To address the unique security challenges of serverless architectures, organizations must implement comprehensive security strategies. Below are key strategies for securing serverless applications.

1. Identity and Access Management (IAM)

Implementing robust identity and access management controls is crucial for securing serverless applications. IAM ensures that only authorized users and services can access specific resources.

- **Least Privilege Principle**: Follow the principle of least privilege when granting permissions to serverless functions and users. Only provide the permissions necessary for a function to perform its intended task.
- **Role-Based Access Control (RBAC)**: Use role-based access control to manage user permissions effectively. Assign roles that group permissions together, making it easier to manage access.

- **Temporary Credentials**: Leverage temporary credentials and short-lived tokens for accessing resources, reducing the risk of credential theft.

2. Secure API Endpoints

APIs are often the primary entry point for serverless applications, making them a key focus for security efforts.

- **Authentication**: Implement strong authentication mechanisms, such as OAuth 2.0 or JSON Web Tokens (JWT), to verify the identity of users and services accessing the API.
- **Authorization**: Enforce authorization checks to ensure that users can only access resources they are permitted to.
- **Rate Limiting and Throttling**: Implement rate limiting and throttling to prevent abuse of API endpoints and mitigate denial-of-service attacks.

3. Input Validation and Data Sanitization

Validating and sanitizing user inputs is crucial for preventing common security vulnerabilities, such as injection attacks.

- **Input Validation**: Validate all incoming data to ensure it meets expected formats, types, and constraints. Reject any input that does not conform to predefined rules.
- **Data Sanitization**: Sanitize user inputs before processing or storing them. This helps prevent injection attacks and data corruption.

4. Secure Function Code and Configuration

The security of serverless functions is paramount. Developers must adhere to secure coding practices and configuration standards.

- **Code Reviews**: Conduct regular code reviews to identify and remediate security vulnerabilities. Ensure that all team members are aware of secure coding practices.
- **Environment Variables**: Use environment variables to store sensitive

information, such as API keys and database credentials. Ensure that these variables are protected and not hard-coded in the function code.

- **Dependencies Management**: Regularly update and audit third-party libraries and dependencies to mitigate known vulnerabilities.

5. Logging and Monitoring

Effective logging and monitoring are essential for detecting security incidents and maintaining visibility into serverless applications.

- **Centralized Logging**: Implement centralized logging to aggregate logs from all serverless functions and services. This allows for easier analysis and monitoring of application activity.
- **Monitoring Tools**: Utilize monitoring tools to track function performance, execution times, and error rates. Set up alerts for suspicious activity or anomalies.
- **Audit Trails**: Maintain audit trails to track access to sensitive resources and actions taken by users. This can help identify potential security incidents.

Best Practices for Security in Serverless Architectures

Implementing security measures in serverless architectures requires adherence to best practices that enhance overall application security. Below are several best practices to consider.

1. Regular Security Assessments

Conduct regular security assessments and penetration testing to identify vulnerabilities in serverless applications. This proactive approach helps organizations stay ahead of potential threats and address weaknesses before they can be exploited.

2. Incident Response Planning

Develop an incident response plan that outlines procedures for detecting, responding to, and recovering from security incidents. Ensure that all team members are familiar with the plan and conduct regular drills to test its effectiveness.

3. Education and Training

Provide ongoing education and training for developers and team members on serverless security best practices. This helps build a security-aware culture within the organization and reduces the likelihood of human error leading to vulnerabilities.

4. Stay Informed About Security Threats

Stay up to date with the latest security threats and vulnerabilities related to serverless architectures. Subscribe to security advisories, blogs, and forums to keep informed about emerging risks and mitigation strategies.

5. Implement Security Automation

Leverage automation tools to streamline security processes, such as vulnerability scanning, configuration checks, and incident response. Automation can help reduce the manual overhead associated with security management and improve response times.

Conclusion

In this chapter, we explored the critical aspects of security in serverless computing, addressing the unique challenges posed by serverless architectures and providing strategies for securing serverless applications. We discussed the shared responsibility model, increased attack surface, lack of visibility, and the complexities introduced by third-party dependencies.

We also examined essential strategies for securing serverless applications, including robust identity and access management, securing API endpoints, input validation, code security, and effective logging and monitoring. By following best practices for security in serverless architectures, organizations can significantly enhance the security posture of their applications.

As we continue our exploration of serverless computing, the next chapters will delve into performance optimization strategies, real-world case studies, and advanced architectural patterns that further enhance the effectiveness of serverless applications.

Chapter 8: Performance Optimization in Serverless Computing

I ntroduction to Performance Optimization in Serverless Architectures

Serverless computing has revolutionized the way applications are built and deployed, offering unprecedented scalability and flexibility. However, the unique characteristics of serverless architectures also introduce specific performance challenges. As businesses increasingly rely on serverless solutions to power their applications, optimizing performance becomes critical to delivering a seamless user experience and maximizing the benefits of serverless computing.

Performance optimization in serverless architectures involves a multi-faceted approach, focusing on reducing latency, optimizing resource usage, and ensuring responsive and efficient applications. This chapter will explore the key strategies for performance optimization, including best practices, common pitfalls, and real-world examples.

Understanding the Performance Characteristics of Serverless

Before diving into optimization strategies, it's essential to understand the unique performance characteristics of serverless architectures.

1. Cold Starts

One of the most significant performance challenges in serverless computing is the phenomenon of "cold starts." When a serverless function is invoked after a period of inactivity, it may take longer to execute due to the time required to provision resources and initialize the execution environment.

- **Impact**: Cold starts can introduce latency, especially for latency-sensitive applications where quick responses are crucial.

2. Statelessness

Serverless functions are inherently stateless, meaning they do not retain any information between invocations. While this design promotes scalability and resilience, it can also lead to performance challenges, particularly when accessing external data stores.

- **Impact**: Each function invocation may require fetching data from external services, potentially increasing response times.

3. Execution Time and Resource Limits

Serverless platforms impose limits on the execution time and resources allocated to functions. Understanding these limits is essential for optimizing performance and avoiding throttling or failures.

- **Impact**: Functions that exceed execution time limits may be terminated, leading to incomplete processing and increased error rates.

4. Integration Latency

Serverless applications often rely on various external services and APIs, which can introduce latency due to network overhead. Understanding the performance characteristics of these integrations is critical for optimizing overall application performance.

- **Impact**: The performance of serverless functions can be significantly affected by the response times of external services.

Key Strategies for Performance Optimization in Serverless

To achieve optimal performance in serverless architectures, organizations can implement several strategies that address the challenges inherent to serverless computing.

1. Minimize Cold Start Latency

Reducing cold start latency is a top priority for optimizing serverless performance. Here are some strategies to consider:

- **Provisioned Concurrency**: Some cloud providers, such as AWS Lambda, offer provisioned concurrency, allowing you to keep a specified number of function instances warm and ready to handle requests. This significantly reduces cold start times.
- **Function Packaging**: Optimize the size of your deployment package by excluding unnecessary libraries, files, and dependencies. Smaller packages lead to faster initialization times.
- **Runtime Selection**: Choose a lightweight runtime for your functions. Some runtimes are faster to initialize than others, which can help reduce cold start latency.
- **Scheduled Warm-Up**: Implement a scheduled warm-up strategy by invoking functions periodically during low-traffic periods to keep them warm and ready for user requests.

2. Optimize Function Execution

To ensure that serverless functions execute efficiently, developers should focus on optimizing code and resource usage.

- **Efficient Code**: Write efficient, modular code that minimizes execution time. Use profiling tools to identify bottlenecks and optimize algorithms.
- **Use Asynchronous Processing**: Where possible, leverage asynchronous processing to allow functions to perform non-blocking operations. This approach enables faster execution and responsiveness.
- **Memory Allocation**: Allocate the appropriate amount of memory to your functions. Serverless platforms often provide more CPU resources as memory increases, so adjusting memory settings can

improve execution speed.

- **Optimize Dependencies**: Minimize the use of large libraries or dependencies. Consider using lighter alternatives or writing custom code to reduce initialization time.

3. Leverage Caching Strategies

Implementing caching can significantly reduce latency and improve performance by minimizing the need to access external data stores.

- **Data Caching**: Use in-memory caches (like AWS ElastiCache or Azure Redis Cache) to store frequently accessed data, reducing the number of calls to external services.
- **Response Caching**: Implement response caching at the API Gateway level to cache responses for specific requests. This reduces the need to invoke backend functions for repeated requests.
- **Cache Invalidation**: Ensure that your caching strategy includes mechanisms for cache invalidation to keep data up to date and prevent stale data from being served.

4. Optimize Data Access Patterns

Efficient data access patterns are crucial for minimizing latency in serverless applications.

- **Batch Processing**: Instead of processing data one item at a time, consider batching multiple items together in a single request. This approach reduces the number of network calls and improves performance.
- **Use Projections**: In applications that implement CQRS, create projections optimized for specific queries to minimize the amount of data that needs to be retrieved.
- **Geographically Distributed Data**: If your application serves users across different regions, consider using geographically distributed data stores to reduce latency. Store data closer to where users are located.

5. Implement Monitoring and Logging

Monitoring and logging are essential for understanding the performance of serverless applications and identifying areas for optimization.

- **Monitoring Tools**: Use monitoring tools like AWS CloudWatch, Azure Monitor, or Google Cloud Operations to track function execution metrics, such as invocation counts, duration, error rates, and throttling incidents.
- **Real-Time Insights**: Implement real-time logging to capture detailed information about function executions. This data can help identify performance bottlenecks and optimize code.
- **Alerting Mechanisms**: Set up alerts for performance-related issues, such as increased error rates or execution time spikes, enabling timely responses to potential problems.

Common Pitfalls in Serverless Performance Optimization

While optimizing performance in serverless architectures, developers should be aware of common pitfalls that can hinder efforts:

1. Over-Optimization

While it's essential to optimize serverless functions, over-optimization can lead to unnecessary complexity. Developers should focus on impactful optimizations rather than getting bogged down in micro-optimizations that provide minimal benefits.

2. Neglecting Monitoring

Failing to implement comprehensive monitoring can result in a lack of visibility into application performance. Without monitoring, identifying performance bottlenecks and optimizing effectively becomes challenging.

3. Ignoring Cost Implications

Performance optimizations can have cost implications, particularly in serverless environments where resource usage directly affects billing. Developers should balance performance improvements with cost considerations, ensuring that optimizations do not lead to unexpected expenses.

4. Inconsistent Testing

Inconsistent testing practices can lead to performance issues that go unnoticed until they impact users. Implement automated testing to evaluate performance under different load conditions and ensure that optimizations are effective.

Real-World Case Studies of Performance Optimization in Serverless

To illustrate the effectiveness of performance optimization strategies in serverless computing, we will explore three real-world case studies that showcase successful implementations.

Case Study 1: E-Commerce Platform

An e-commerce platform leveraging AWS Lambda faced performance challenges due to cold starts and high latency during peak shopping seasons. To address these issues, the development team implemented the following strategies:

- **Provisioned Concurrency**: The team enabled provisioned concurrency for critical Lambda functions, ensuring that a certain number of instances were always warm during peak traffic.
- **Data Caching**: The team integrated AWS ElastiCache to cache frequently accessed product information, reducing the number of calls to the database.
- **Monitoring**: They implemented AWS CloudWatch monitoring to track function performance and set up alerts for increased execution times.

Results: The e-commerce platform experienced a 50% reduction in average response time, improved user experience during peak shopping events, and reduced costs by minimizing database read requests.

Case Study 2: Real-Time Analytics Application

A real-time analytics application built on Google Cloud Functions required low latency for processing incoming data streams. To optimize performance, the team employed the following strategies:

- **Asynchronous Processing**: The application architecture was designed to process incoming data asynchronously, allowing functions to respond quickly to events without blocking execution.

- **Geographically Distributed Data**: The team utilized Google Firestore, with data stored in multiple regions to minimize latency for users across different geographical locations.
- **Batch Processing**: Incoming data was processed in batches, reducing the number of write operations to Firestore and improving overall throughput.

Results: The application achieved sub-second latency for data processing, significantly enhancing the user experience and allowing real-time insights.

Case Study 3: Social Media Application

A social media application using Azure Functions faced performance challenges due to high volumes of user-generated content. To improve performance, the development team implemented the following:

- **API Management**: The team leveraged Azure API Management to manage API requests and implement rate limiting to protect backend services.
- **Response Caching**: They utilized Azure Redis Cache to store frequently accessed user profiles and posts, reducing the load on Azure Functions.
- **Function Optimization**: The team conducted code reviews and optimizations, focusing on minimizing execution time and memory usage for each function.

Results: The social media application saw a 30% reduction in API response times, improved user engagement, and a more efficient backend architecture.

Conclusion

In this chapter, we explored the critical aspects of performance optimization in serverless computing. We examined the unique performance characteristics of serverless architectures, including cold starts, statelessness, execution time limits, and integration latency.

We discussed key strategies for optimizing performance, such as minimizing cold start latency, optimizing function execution, leveraging caching, improving data access patterns, and implementing effective monitoring and logging.

Additionally, we highlighted common pitfalls to avoid during optimization efforts and provided real-world case studies to illustrate successful performance optimization strategies in serverless applications.

As we continue our exploration of serverless computing, the next chapters will focus on advanced topics such as cost optimization, effective deployment strategies, and best practices for scaling serverless applications to meet increasing demands.

Chapter 10

Chapter 11

Chapter 12